thecaseworkjournal.
If it's not written; then it didn't happen.

Avid Solutions, LLC

Copyright © 2016 Avid Solutions, LLC

All rights reserved.

ISBN: ISBN-13:978-0692723449

ISBN-10:0692723447

thecaseworkjournal

Avid Solutions, LLC

Dedication

This book is dedicated to the human service professionals who have made the commitment to servicing vulnerable individuals and families. It is through your care and dedication that children continue to be safe and families gain opportunities to lead productive lives. Words alone will never express how much you are appreciated. We offer you our gratitude, respect and admiration for a job well done.

Sherie Burgess, Executive Director & Founder
-Avid Solutions, LLC

Avid Solutions, LLC

Preface

Documentation is often the least glamorous part of the human service profession. Despite this fact, how and what is documented often becomes the most important aspect of the job. At a minimum, documentation evaluates progress, provides tools for supervision, operates as a guide in the absence of the worker, functions as a legal record in court and details how decisions are made.

Recognizing the vast need to provide human service professionals with the resources to complete clear, concise and accurate documentation, we at Avid Solutions, LLC, have spent years working alongside front line workers and supervisors in developing the training *"Casework Documentation"* and its companion, *"thecaseworkjournal"*. Our primary objective is to make the practice of social work more effective by streamlining best practice procedures that will make the job more organized, reliable and above all, simpler.

Avid Solutions, LLC

Notes to consider:

"If it's not written, then it did not happened!"

Avid Solutions, LLC

Notes to consider:

> "Don't let your struggle become your identity."
>
> -Raltson Bowles

Notes to consider:

> "Your job is not to judge. Your job is not to figure out if someone deserves something. Your job is to lift the fallen, to restore the broken and to heal the hurting." –Joel Osteen

Avid Solutions, LLC

Notes to consider:

> "If it was easy, then everyone would do it." -Unknown

Notes to consider:

> "Life is a camera, Focus on what's important, Capture the good times, Develop from the negatives; and if things don't work out, take another shot."
> -Unknown

Notes to consider:

"You can't make this stuff up!"

Notes to consider:

"You are helpful…….and a little nosey."

Notes to consider:

"Treat people as if they were what they ought to be and you will help them to become what they are capable of becoming."
–Johann Wolfagang Van Goethl

Notes to consider:

"It is what it is!"

Avid Solutions, LLC

Notes to consider:

> "Be a warrior, not a worrier."
> -Unknown

Notes to consider:

"Ever have a situation where all you can say is, *REALLY?*"

Avid Solutions, LLC

Notes to consider:

> "Work for the cause; not for the applause."
> -Unknown

Notes to consider:

"Wondering if you picked the wrong major in college?"

Avid Solutions, LLC

Notes to consider:

> "You will feel fulfilled when you do the impossible for someone else." -Unknown

Notes to consider:

"The greatest tool you have is to listen." -Unknown

Avid Solutions, LLC

Notes to consider:

> "Motivation is what gets you started. Habit is what keeps you going." –Jim Rohn

Notes to consider:

"Don't count the minutes, count the laughs." -Unknown

Notes to consider:

"Don't cling to a mistake just because you spent a lot of time making it." -Unknown

Notes to consider:

"You are not responsible for fixing everything that is broken." -Unknown

Avid Solutions, LLC

Notes to consider:

> "Self-care is not selfish, and saying NO doesn't make you bad person." -Unknown

Notes to consider:

> "Never think that what you have to offer is insignificant. There will always be someone out there that needs what you have to give." -Unknown

Avid Solutions, LLC

Notes to consider:

> "Be the kind of worker you would like to have."
> –Unknown

Notes to consider:

> "Recognize and address your feelings. Don't take hostile statements personally."

Notes to consider:

> "Your life is a message to share with the world. Make sure it is inspiring."
> -Unknown

Notes to consider:

> "Practice empathy and try to imagine walking in the shoes of others." -Unknown

PERSONAL REFLECTIONS.......

-
-
-
-
-
-
-
-
-
-
-
-
-
-
-
-
-
-
-
-
-
-
-
-
-
-
-
-
-

Avid Solutions, LLC

Notes to consider:

> "Meet clients where they are. If they are not ready, no change will occur."

Notes to consider:

"Document, Document, Document!"

Avid Solutions, LLC

Notes to consider:

> "Keep your head up and keep your heart strong." -Unknown

Notes to consider:

"If it feels wrong, don't do it."

Avid Solutions, LLC

Notes to consider:

> "Say what you mean, just don't say it mean."

Notes to consider:

"Ever have one of those days where all you can say is UGH?"

Avid Solutions, LLC

Notes to consider:

> "If serving is below you then leadership is beyond you."
> -Unknown

Notes to consider:

"So far you've survived 100% of your worst days." -Unknown

Avid Solutions, LLC

Notes to consider:

"You are where you are supposed to be. If you weren't, then you wouldn't be there."

Notes to consider:

> "Don't lose hope. You never know what tomorrow will bring." -Unknown

Avid Solutions, LLC

Notes to consider:

"Today may have been the day to stay in bed."

thecaseworkjournal

Notes to consider:

> "Sometimes you have to forget what's gone, appreciate what still remains and look forward to what is coming next."
> -Unknown

Avid Solutions, LLC

Notes to consider:

> "Be the person that someone looks at and say because of you I didn't give up." -Unknown

Notes to consider:

> "You are capable of amazing things." -Unknown

Avid Solutions, LLC

Notes to consider:

> "To make a difference in someone's life, you don't have to be brilliant, rich, beautiful or perfect. You just have to care."
> –Mandy Hale

Notes to consider:

> "Have patience with those you serve and with yourself."

Avid Solutions, LLC

Notes to consider:

> "Help people even when you know they can't help you back." -Unknown

Notes to consider:

> "Clients should be able to read the notes and think it's a fair representation of them."

Avid Solutions, LLC

Notes to consider:

> "I'm not telling you it is going to be easy, I'm telling you it's going to be worth it." -Unknown

Notes to consider:

"Never stop doing your best just because someone doesn't give you credit." -Unknown

Avid Solutions, LLC

Notes to consider:

> "Don't allow yourself to get fatigued doing good. At the right time it will harvest a good crop if you don't give up or quit." -Unknown

Notes to consider:

> "Your greatness is not what you have, it is what you give." –Alice Hocker

Notes to consider:

> "Sometimes a mental health day is needed, maybe even two."

Notes to consider:

"Think about what you are going to write before you begin."

Avid Solutions, LLC

Notes to consider:

> "Forgive! Even when it is hard."
> -Unknown

PERSONAL REFLECTIONS............

-
-
-
-
-
-
-
-
-
-
-
-
-
-
-
-
-
-
-
-
-
-
-
-
-
-
-
-
-

Avid Solutions, LLC

"You know the elevator doesn't work, right?"

Notes to consider:

> "You have two hands, one to help yourself and the second to help others." -Unknown

Avid Solutions, LLC

Notes to consider:

> "Don't give up on anybody.
> Miracles happen every day."
> -Unknown

Notes to consider:

> "Try and leave people better than how you found them."
> -Unknown

Avid Solutions, LLC

Notes to consider:

> "Remember that guy who gave up? ....
> Neither does anyone else."
> - Unknown

Notes to consider:

> "We are defined by our actions toward others not others actions toward us." -Unknown

Notes to consider:

> "You can always do more than you think you can."
> –John Wooden

Notes to consider:

> "Even if you quit, they will probably still ask for the progress notes."

Notes to consider:

> "Every worker has that one client that will be remembered forever."

Notes to consider:

"Some days all you can do is smile and keep moving."

Avid Solutions, LLC

Notes to consider:

> "There will be no crisis today. Your schedule is already full."
>
> -Unknown

Notes to consider:

> "Never underestimate your ability to make someone else's life better; even if you never know about it."
> -Greg Louganis

Avid Solutions, LLC

Notes to consider:

> "I do this for the money," said by no social worker ever.
> -Unknown

Notes to consider:

"Relax……….You can't control everything."

Avid Solutions, LLC

Notes to consider:

> "Better days are coming; they are called Saturdays and Sundays." - Unknown

Notes to consider:

> "Develop your intuition and trust your gut."

Avid Solutions, LLC

Notes to consider:

"Learn how to decline offers of food or other refreshments tactfully."

Notes to consider:

> "Live for something higher, bigger and better than you."
> -Unknown

Notes to consider:

> "Say it straight and with a smile." - Unknown

Notes to consider:

_____

_____

_____

_____

_____

_____

_____

> "You were born with the ability to help someone improve their life."

_____

_____

_____

_____

_____

_____

_____

_____

_____

_____

_____

_____

_____

Avid Solutions, LLC

Notes to consider:

> "Alone we can do so little; together we can do so much."
> –Helen Kellar

Notes to Consider:

> "Don't wait for others. Pat yourself on the back for a job well done."

Avid Solutions, LLC

Notes to consider:

"One of the hardest things you will do in life is to help people, who don't know they need help."

Notes to consider:

> "Everyone you meet has something to teach you."
> -Unknown

Avid Solutions, LLC

Notes to consider:

> "Your job is hard. You are entitled to a moment; just don't stay there too long."

PERSONAL REFLECTIONS.......

-
-
-
-
-
-
-
-
-
-
-
-
-
-
-
-
-
-
-
-
-
-
-
-
-
-
-
-

Avid Solutions, LLC

Notes to consider:

"You can't fix all of their problems but you can help them face their problems."
-Unknown

Notes to consider:

> "Focus on what matters."
> -Unknown

Notes to consider:

> "It's a slow process but quitting won't speed it up."
> -Unknown

Avid Solutions, LLC

Notes to consider:

"Might be time for that break."

thecaseworkjournal

Notes to consider:

"You are how you work."

Avid Solutions, LLC

Notes to consider:

> "Don't be discouraged. It's often the last key in the bunch that opens the lock."
> -Unknown

Notes to consider:

"You can and You Will."
-Unknown

Avid Solutions, LLC

Notes to consider:

> "You can't fix crazy. All you can do is document it."
> -Unknown

Notes to consider:

> "Compliment people; magnify their strengths not their weakness." -Unknown

Avid Solutions, LLC

Notes to consider:

"Know your client population."

Notes to consider:

"There are days when it's just too much and all you can do is take a couple of deep breaths."

Avid Solutions, LLC

Notes to consider:

> "Don't be pushed by your problems; be led by your dreams."
> -Ralph Waldo Emerson

Notes to consider:

"You are amazing. You are brave. You are Strong."
-Unknown

Avid Solutions, LLC

Notes to consider:

> "The dream is free but the hustle is sold separately."
> -Unknown

Notes to consider:

"Not today!"

Avid Solutions, LLC

Notes to consider:

> "Personal information should only be shared if it benefits the client."

Notes to consider:

> "Safety is never negotiable for you or the client."

Notes to consider:

> "Next time you feel stressed; just start laughing."

Notes to consider:

> "Have clear and realistic expectations for yourself and the clients."

Avid Solutions, LLC

Notes to consider:

> "If it doesn't make sense to you, it won't make sense to anyone else."

Notes to consider:

> "Use your super powers for good."

Avid Solutions, LLC

Notes to consider:

"Clients have the best stories but H.I.P.P.A prohibits sharing."
–Unknown

Notes to consider:

"Feel great, act great and be great." - Unknown

Notes to consider:

"Seriously, a pay raise would be nice."

Notes to consider:

_____
_____
_____
_____
_____
_____
_____

> "Inspire others to help those in need." -Unknown

_____
_____
_____
_____
_____
_____
_____
_____
_____
_____
_____
_____

Avid Solutions, LLC

PERSONAL REFLECTIONS............

- _____
- _____
- _____
- _____
- _____
- _____
- _____
- _____
- _____
- _____
- _____
- _____
- _____
- _____
- _____
- _____
- _____
- _____
- _____
- _____
- _____
- _____
- _____
- _____
- _____
- _____

thecaseworkjournal

"They forgot to give me the instructions for it."

Avid Solutions, LLC

Notes to consider:

> "You can't live a positive life with a negative mind."
> -Joyce Meyers

Notes to consider:

> "People will forget what you said, people will forget what you did, but people will never forget how you made them feel." – Maya Angelou

Notes to consider:

> "Strong people stand up for themselves but the strongest people stand up for others."
> –Nishan Panwar

Notes to consider:

"Keep up the good work."

Avid Solutions, LLC

Notes to consider.

> "Take a deep breath and try again tomorrow."

thecaseworkjournal

Notes to consider:

> "A simple hello could lead to a million wonderful things."
> -Unknown

Notes to consider:

"There are 7 days in the week and someday isn't one of them." -Unknown

Notes to consider:

"Sometimes less is more."
-Unknown

Avid Solutions, LLC

Notes to consider:

> "The only real mistake is the one from which we learn nothing." Unknown

Notes to consider:

"There is no elevator to success. You have to take the stairs." -Unknown

Avid Solutions, LLC

Notes to consider:

> "The difference between *"try"* and *"triumph"* is a little *"umph."* –Marvin Phillips

Notes to consider:

> "If you want something you've never had, you have to do something you've never done."
> -Unknown

Notes to consider:

> "Trust yourself! You know more than you think you do."
> -Unknown

Notes to consider:

> "Sometimes the hardest thing and the right thing are the same." -Unknown

Avid Solutions, LLC

Notes to consider:

> "Don't wait for people to be friendly, show them how."
> -Unknown

Notes to consider:

"If Plan A didn't work, there are 25 more letters in the alphabet."
–Kane Arreo

Notes to consider:

> "There are entirely too many cases and too much paperwork."

thecaseworkjournal

Notes to consider:

"Being right is over-rated."

Avid Solutions, LLC

Notes to consider:

> "Inspiring others towards happiness brings you happiness." -Unknown

Notes to consider:

> "The meaning of life is to find your gift. The purpose of life is to give it away." —Unknown

Avid Solutions, LLC

Notes to consider:

> "Think about why you started this job in the first place."
> -Unknown

Notes to consider:

"Everything is okay in the end. If it's not okay, then it's not the end." -Unknown

Avid Solutions, LLC

Notes to consider:

> "Appreciate yourself and honor your soul." -Unknown

Notes to consider:

"I know that it has been tough but I'm still cheering for you."
-Unknown

Notes to consider:

> "You are allowed to be both a masterpiece and a work in progress simultaneously."
> –Sophia Bush

PERSONAL REFLECTIONS............

-
-
-
-
-
-
-
-
-
-
-
-
-
-
-
-
-
-
-
-
-
-
-
-
-

Avid Solutions, LLC

Notes to consider:

> "Strength does not lie in what you have. It lies in what you give." –Unknown

Notes to consider:

"You were born to do more than just go to work, pay bills and die." -Unknown

Notes to consider:

> "You cannot direct the wind but you can adjust the sails."
> **Unknown**

Avid Solutions, LLC

Notes to consider:

> "Set clear boundaries at the start of every relationship. Revisit and re-define them as needed."

Notes to consider:

> "Let your smile change the world but don't let the world change your smile." -Unknown

Avid Solutions, LLC

Notes to consider:

> "Strive for progress, not perfection." -Unknown

Notes to consider:

> "Mondays come entirely too quick."

Avid Solutions, LLC

Notes to consider:

> "There is no substitute for hard work." –Thomas Edison

Notes to consider:

> "Well Done is better than Well Said." –Benjamin Franklin

Notes to consider:

> "Be a hand that reaches out. Be a smile for those who have no reason to smile. Be a light for those who live in darkness."
> -Unknown

Notes to consider:

> "You cannot do everything but you can do something."
> -Unknown

Notes to consider:

> "Nothing can be learned while you are talking." -Unknown

Notes to consider:

> "Live in such a way that if someone spoke badly about you; no one would believe it."
> –Unknown

Avid Solutions, LLC

Notes to consider:

> "The person who says it cannot be done should not interrupt the person who is doing it."
> –Chinese Proverb

Notes to consider:

> "You can nurture a child by strengthening the family."
> –Unknown

Avid Solutions, LLC

Notes to consider:

> "Stand for what you believe in even if it means you stand alone." –Unknown

Notes to consider:

"You got this!"

Avid Solutions, LLC

Notes to consider:

"No matter how you feel; get up, dress up, show up and never give up". –Regina Brett

Notes to consider:

"Your work speaks to who you are."

Avid Solutions, LLC

Notes to consider:

> "You don't need a reason to help people." –Unknown

Notes to consider:

"Don't ruin a good today by thinking about a bad yesterday. Let it go!" –Unknown

Notes to consider:

> "Identify and use social supports to prevent burnout and stress."

Notes to consider:

> "Worrying doesn't take away tomorrow's trouble, it takes away today's peace." -Unknown

Avid Solutions, LLC

Notes to consider:

"The work you do is important. Take it seriously!"

PERSONAL REFLECTIONS............

- _____
- _____
- _____
- _____
- _____
- _____
- _____
- _____
- _____
- _____
- _____
- _____
- _____
- _____
- _____
- _____
- _____
- _____
- _____
- _____
- _____
- _____
- _____
- _____
- _____
- _____

Avid Solutions, LLC

Group in Session.

Notes to consider:

"Recharge your batteries and keep going."

Avid Solutions, LLC

Notes to consider:

"Don't forget you are human."

Notes to consider:

"Have the meltdown, just don't unpack and live there."
-Unknown

Avid Solutions, LLC

Notes to consider:

"The things you are passionate about are not random; they are your calling."
–Fabienne Fredrickson

Notes to consider:

> "Listen with the intent to understand not with the intent to reply." –Stephen Convey

Avid Solutions, LLC

Notes to consider:

"Sometimes the people with the worst past end up creating the best future." -Unknown

Notes to consider:

> "Character is how you treat people who can do nothing for you." –Ramandeep Singh

Avid Solutions, LLC

Notes to consider:

"Be brave; even if you're not, pretend to be, no one can tell the difference." -Unknown

Notes to consider:

"Do what is right not what is easy." –Unknown

Avid Solutions, LLC

Notes to consider:

"In case no one told you today, Thank you."

Notes to consider:

> "Unless someone like you cares a whole lot, nothing is going to get better." –Unknown

Notes to consider:

"Keep putting out good. It will come back to you tenfold in unexpected ways."
–Farrah Gray

Notes to consider:

> "If you are going to do something do it right the first time." –Unknown

Notes to consider:

"Be somebody who makes everybody feel like somebody."
-Unknown

Notes to consider:

> "Be strong, but not rude. Be kind, but not weak. Be bold, but not a bully. Be proud, but not arrogant." –Unknown

Notes to consider:

"Realize how good you really are." –Unknown

Notes to consider:

"Be mindful of the professional clients."

Avid Solutions, LLC

Notes to consider:

> "Be kind! Everyone you meet is fighting a battle you know nothing about." -Unknown

Notes to Consider:

> "Do your little bit of good where you are." -Unknown

Avid Solutions, LLC

Notes to Consider:

> "Be the reason someone smiles today." -Unknown

Notes to Consider:

"You only fail when you stop trying." -Unknown

Avid Solutions, LLC

Notes to consider:

> "We learn something through everyone that passes through our lives. Some lessons are painful, some lessons are painless and some lessons are priceless." -Unknown

Notes to consider:

"Work hard and be nice to people."

Avid Solutions, LLC

Notes to consider:

"It's not about being the best. It's about being better than you were yesterday." -Unknown

Notes to consider:

"I am thankful for my job!"

"I am thankful for my job!"

"I am thankful for my job!"

Avid Solutions, LLC

PERSONAL REFLECTIONS............

thecaseworkjournal

"If not you, then who?"

Avid Solutions, LLC

Notes to consider:

> "Take care of yourself so people get the best of you and not what's left of you."
> –Carl Bryan

Notes to consider:

> "You are going to make a difference. A lot of times it won't be huge, or even visible; but it will matter just the same."
> -Unknown

Avid Solutions, LLC

Notes to consider:

> "Have you smiled at someone today?"
> -Unknown

Notes to consider:

> "It's okay if the only thing you did today was breathe."
> -Unknown

Avid Solutions, LLC

Notes to consider:

> "You and your clients are <u>NOT</u> friends."

Notes to consider:

> "Learn to listen. Sometimes opportunity knocks very softly."
> –H. Jackson Brown Jr.

Notes to consider:

> "Life doesn't get easier. You just get stronger." -Unknown

Notes to consider:

> "Do not let what you can't do interfere with what you can do."
> -Unknown

Avid Solutions, LLC

Notes to consider:

> "If you are persistent you will get it. If you are consistent you will keep it." -Unknown

Notes to consider:

"A positive attitude may not solve all your problems, but it annoys enough people to make it worthwhile." –Herb Albright

Avid Solutions, LLC

Notes to consider:

"Mistakes are proof you are trying." -Unknown

Notes to consider:

"Advocating does not mean doing it for clients."

Notes to consider:

> "You can't pour from an empty cup. Take care of yourself first." -Unknown

Notes to consider:

> "Sometimes it's other people and sometimes it's you."

Avid Solutions, LLC

Notes to consider:

"Be clear, honest and direct with your clients."

Notes to consider:

"Let go of trying to control other's people's behavior."

Avid Solutions, LLC

Notes to consider:

"Hug your own sh%#"

Notes to consider:

"Every day is a new day to make a positive impact on someone's life." -Unknown

Avid Solutions, LLC

Notes to consider:

> "Learn more than others; work more than others but expect less than others." -Unknown

Notes to consider:

> "You should not be working harder than the clients for THEIR goals."

Avid Solutions, LLC

Notes to consider:

> "Because of you, someone laughed a little harder, cried a little less, and smiled a little more." -Unknown

Notes to consider:

> "First take care of yourself then you can take care of the world."
> -Unknown

Notes to Consider:

> "Every day may not be good, but there's something good in every day." -Unknown

thecaseworkjournal

Notes to Consider:

> "Whether you think you can or you think you can't, you are right." –Henry Ford

Notes to consider:

> "Thank you for all your hard work. It and you are sincerely appreciated."

PERSONAL REFLECTIONS............

- _____
- _____
- _____
- _____
- _____
- _____
- _____
- _____
- _____
- _____
- _____
- _____
- _____
- _____
- _____
- _____
- _____
- _____
- _____
- _____
- _____
- _____
- _____
- _____
- _____
- _____
- _____

ABOUT THE AUTHOR

Sherie Burgess is an LMSW with over fifteen years of experience working with diverse populations including children, homeless people, substance abusers, survivors of domestic violence, and the elderly. Sherie received her BS in Social Work from Morgan State University and went on to earn a Master's Degree from the University of Maryland, Baltimore School for Social Work.

thecaseworkjournal

www.ingramcontent.com/pod-product-compliance
Lightning Source LLC
Chambersburg PA
CBHW020852090426
42736CB00008B/342